Desire Lines

Desire Lines
Glen Downie

Wolsak and Wynn . Toronto

Typeset in Goudy, printed in Canada by The Coach House Printing Company, Toronto, Ontario

Author's photograph: Emma Downie
Cover photographs: Glen Downie
Cover design: Coach House

Some of these poems first appeared in *Crucible, Event, The New Quarterly, Paperplates, Pottersfield Portfolio, Queen's Quarterly, Scrivener, Split Shift,* and *sub-Terrain.* 'Black Thread' was previously published in *Wishbone Dance* (Wolsak & Wynn, 1999).

The publishers gratefully acknowledge the support of the Canada Council for the Arts and the Ontario Arts Council.

Wolsak and Wynn Publishers Ltd
192 Spadina Avenue, Suite 315
Toronto, ON
Canada M5T 2C2

National Library of Canada Cataloguing in Publication Data

Downie, Glen,
        Desire lines / Glen Downie.

Poems.
ISBN 0-919897-84-3

I. Title.

PS8557.O84D48 2002   C811'.54   C2002-903164-8
PR9199.3.D615D48 2002

ACKNOWLEDGEMENTS

For hospitalities en route,
thanks to Phil, Jane & Brett; Max, Monica & Fiona; Ross;
& Allison

For financial assistance,
thanks to *Books in Canada* & The Ontario Arts Council

For timely encouragement,
thanks to David Zieroth

Contents

Beginning

Muddle

End

Notes

Beginning

*Time put back — it sounded good but what does it come to in reality?
Does anyone here get time at full value, a true time, a time cut off from
a fresh bolt of cloth, smelling of newness and dye? Quite the contrary.
It is used-up time, worn out by other people, a shabby time full of holes,
like a sieve.*

— Bruno Schulz

Cliché Europe

:a trek I'd been ducking since I was 20

when *everyone* backpacked through Europe strolling
down the Cliché Elysées   smack
into the same high school glad-hands
they'd just shaken off
I gathered the moss of a

beard & wrote a suicide
paper   imagined that Psych
might teach me my cliché
self   The prof smirked
through his dope fog & said I'd do better
hiking cliché Europe

Sixteen years later   after our spitfight
the boss tells me I've *always had trouble
accepting authority*   suggests I consider my future
in the department   I shoot him

glances over my shoulder as I run desperate   a cliché
salaryman fleeing Godzilla   mouth moving
out of sync with dubbed terror   *What would you do*

the staff safety quiz wants to know *if
your clothing caught fire
right now?*   Good question!   Meanwhile   we're locked
in a living-together cliché
having misjudged wounded failed begrudged

hunkered down for lonely-togetherness given
compassion away in our work taken on its wounds
her autism my cancer

Having stretched ourselves thin
as El Greco portraits   we elect to ignore
the unsought advice about pickpockets bad hotels
surly Frenchmen crooked cabbies Eiffel
towers made in Hong Kong & grasp instead
the straw of tired promises
each other's   the travel agent's:

a break
with routine   renewal
of yr love life   satisfaction
guaranteed or money
gleefully refunded   the holiday you'll never
forget & the gimcracks for when you do   Time
& Timelessness
immanence & transcendence   history
& its near relative
histrionics   Argue in The Eternal
City – put a real
scrap in yr travel scrapbook

Phil writes that it's pissing
on Crete   They're stir-crazy
with a new baby & starved
for visitors   Staring dumbly
at cliché Europe   other pinpoints appear
Max in Bern   Ross in Paris   stars
of an unconsidered constellation   The rest
we can make up as we go   it's
time we embraced
the cliché & let whatever happens
happen

Muddle

If you step forward with your right foot, you see your left foot move ...
Not only does "left" become "right", but "up" becomes "down", the ceiling
becomes the floor. To achieve this, circumstances must be favourable
and you must be prepared to practice and look with an open mind.

– M.C. Escher

History's Radio

Flight: the long homeless moment
before we touch
down   the late
dog-tired wait
by the sad carousel

for the dead weight of our lives
to come round & claim us   We miss
the last bus   feel
our bodies speed away
in a cab while our minds are still
churning the last day of work
& the stove – did we remember
the stove?   The papers
all Greek to me now   I lose

interest in the new   having landed
in the past   the Acropolis
visible   I hunch   from
our hotel roof   I leave you

asleep & sneak up there
my body jet-lagging behind
this instinct   only
the jolt of night air forestalling
total system failure   Alone

above the city   my shivering subsides
as the Parthenon's dawn-touched stones
become live coals   its glowing
columns the tubes of a warming-up
radio   history's radio
-active bones

Faith in postcards

There is nothing to look at any more,
Everything has been seen to death.
　　　　　　　　　　　　　　　　　– D. H. Lawrence

what naïveté made us each believe
we'd be the only one

waiting on sunset at this church
Instamatic　Canon
-wielding pilgrims　cursing
each other's burned heads
for intruding into *our* shot

how desperate this need
for static
full-frontal
meaning
the stock photographic answer
the definitive angle

that will say THIS *is Greece*
when it's only the lip
of one blown volcano

how shabby this faith
in the arrogant postcard

Black thread

To leave behind the silencing
cancers & wander
a geography of voices

To put my ear to the very ground
where the poem is rooted
& hear Homer's oration

To follow him   the blind
leading the blind   among
islands warm to the touch

back to my own
century & find you on Crete
quoting Elytis

       *   *   *

Among the olive groves & unfaltering sun you ask
for home news   Reluctant
I bring the dark word
of your editor's illness
A tumour in the mouth & she too a poet
Then come the usual questions

Times like these
what wouldn't I give to be someone
else   Kirsten or Kate   & be asked
how to bathe a baby or frame a house
instead of the inevitable

What are her chances? Is treatment
hell? My sad expertise
shadows me even here a black thread
for friends to pull on
unravelling fears

      *   *   *

My years at the clinic: too many
voices lost   tongues tied
by tumour   lips cut
& crookedly closed
dimpled unbeautifully
at the cigarette's perching place
No respecter of persons cancer
& cruel in its ironies blackening
humour with blows to basic functions
defining capacities
       His speech distorted
       by surgery & an ill-fitting denture
       Doktor Freud father of "the talking cure"
       tells his Parisian visitors
       My prosthesis doesn't speak French
       he pries open his teeth with a clothes peg
       to smoke his cigars

       Richard Blessing cursed
       with tumour & graced with
       poetry examines his own brain scan

& metaphorizes – the convoluted
lobes *are* truly walnuts

& Villa-Lobos   asked
in his last months "Are you composing?"
replies ruefully *No –*
decomposing

However darkened   poetry & song
endure   To the end   even beyond   Let us remember this
we who are sound

   * * *

Weeks later   I sail off into Eco's
essays   hike the novels of Dürrenmatt
take the night train to the heart
of Machado's poems   I'm transported
by national voices   the journey's
a run-on sentence in many languages
I miss the glottochronology but not the root
-words   the common threads:
speranza esperanza espoir ...
I send you a bright postcard
& *sotto voce* a prayer
between the lines:

Let cancer never translate her
into silence   How would we know
we've come home
without her voice?

Beached

Ear to the ground but
not listening –

I keep my head down
eyes closed I've had enough

contention *Always had trouble*
accepting authority

A babe in the cradle
of democracy   I'm beached

sweating out the political
juices wanting only to drift on seas of
blue timelessness to dive deep

emerging innocent living as if
this island were without masters
& had skilfully disinvented
radio TV

When the tanks roll into
Tien'anmen Square I know nothing
think nothing Enough

contention! Ear to the ground but not
listening I doze for weeks before
tremors reach me
as another Godzilla nightmare

                              But this time
someone has declined to run
stands & stares down the beast
Into my ear   history
rumbles its wake-up call

Fragmentary

Greek light startles
the retina   retsina
startles the palate   The landscape's
palette all sun-baked earth tones

except for white churches & houses
except for blue sea & sky
How beautiful the dirty

potsherd islands against such brilliance

    *   *   *

Minds reel in the heat   Hard climb
up the rubble road
the coarse brush overgrown
good tinder for the hanged apostle's
Easter bonfire

Somewhere ahead   splashes
of watery music   invisible
orchestra   Then one by one
the belled & shaggy goats

The hanged man

Easter on Crete:
out of place
& just where I need to be

The Sunday School perfect-attender
comes up empty
trying to recall a lesson on penance
instructions for rebirth

The vestigial faith
of childhood
demands something

perhaps this Greek liturgy   impenetrable
except as deep
old sound

a long homeless moment
when the priest takes away
the light of the world

leaving us
with our sins   This much

I grasp without language
with the claw of bad conscience

   * * *

The heart waits in the foreign tomb
of ritual

pressed close by black-dressed
fishermen & farmers

for the end of grief
for bodily resurrection

for an alleluia
that will not be lost
in translation

The priest disappears behind a screen
the barrel-shaped church goes black

Outside   Judas
swings in the night breeze   a pendulum
ticking Death-time   We lie in the grave
of our guilt
stone-separated
from love

The priest emerges with a candle: hope
& a torch for the hanged man

what would you do
if your clothing caught fire
right now

Kids dance round the traitor & laugh
tossing firecrackers up to the bell

which enlarges each pop
to a Big Bang   creates
from a small village rite
a triumph over death & despair   which
echoes long after we turn home

Humblessed: The plainsong of Francis and Poor Clare

A homily on humility:
Assisi tiles its roofs
with broken hearts

their halves laid curve
over curve undulating
rows of soft rose-brown

(dust of perpetual poverty
stained with the blood of stigmata)

while rank on rank of olive trees
maintain a monastic separateness

while the laity of sunflowers crowd together
their upturned faces
a choir of praise

to chant a plainsong
of echoed colour & form
(what strengthens the soul
bears repeating)
to slow the heart   lower
the pressure
of this life

as the swaths of mowed fields   blind
to the subtle fruits of
their own faithless pilgrimage
move away in apple-green
& return in emerald

Mussolini slept here

Mussolini slept here
with his mistress   They issue us clean sheets
to be changed on Sunday & insist
we sleep apart   Down the men's wing I wander
clutching my bridal-white linen   A naked man
crossing from the shower sneezes
& a piano somewhere fires a volley of chords
In the empty hall   the sounds echo a long time

Near the heart of Florence *Cinema Edison*
offers a poster-sized kiss   (They loved
escapist musicals   & the propaganda
pumped from Il Duce's studio)   Piazzo
Tomasso Edison's a leisurely stroll from
his villa (now hostel) where movies
begin at 20 past 8   Last night
Alien   Tonight it's
Trading Places

'Tomasso' Edison was born in Milan
Ohio   a cousin   I'm told   to my great-grandmother
Fellow named Ott worked for him   funny guy
whose party trick was sneezing on command
Record of a Sneeze became one of the first
moving pictures   In another   two men waltz
while a third plays the fiddle
To display such things   even for half a minute
was nickel magic near the end of the nineteenth century

A few doors away   Ross practices
piano   It's Winnipeg   early '60s
Italian soccer on short wave   my mother evasive
on just how babies are made   He says
She has to tell you   It's her job   Inside
the kinetoscope   men hold each other
dancing   *Orgasm* they tell kids now
is like a sneeze

Ross will meet us in Paris   For the moment
we're in the dark   It's 8:19   We're Canadian
German   American
British   French   Swiss
Argentinean   Japanese ...
Aliens   trading places all summer long

In '45   they shot Benito
& Claretta   strung them up with
piano wire at a gas station in Milan
The man plants a seed my mother finally told me
They have to love each other very much

Sensuous distance: Marco Polo in Venice

1271

The man plants a seed   & promptly leaves her
pregnant   What manner of man
would do that?   One such as
my father   Flight   his long homeless moment
lasted fifteen years   Returned to find his wife
dead & the son he'd never seen
almost a man   Was he fleeing me
or my mother or the labyrinth
of Venice?   I ask   what manner of man
is Nicolo Polo?

*   *   *

A merchant   Aunt Flora had said
an adventurous trader   When he returns
he'll bring you the gifts of travel
Orphaned by travel   what olive branch
would appease me?   The man plants a seed: myself
that itch for leaving   My father traded our port
for perpetual voyage

*   *   *

The docks my rude school where everyone shouts
the lessons of coin & water: fortunes
are fluid   wealth is
always moving   In the shell game of commerce

sandalwood becomes cinnamon   silks turn to pearls
ginger to ivory   Merchants have taught me everything
has a price   Slavers weigh lives against
rubies or cotton   An English sailor asks:
What manner of man is your father?
Trying his tongue   I answer him: *traitor*
trader

             *   *   *

Over the Roof of the World   he followed the Silk Road
to Cathay   & the court of Kubla Khan
Drawn   he says   not by gold alone
but by all that lies beyond
the Biblical map: far east of Eden   past
the four rivers of Paradise –
the unknown
that incomparable spice that must be tasted

Like an unwound ribbon of silk
a curve of water
snakes through the heart of Venice
a sensuous distance

such as a man may love & yet
leave for another   This man   this stranger
offers no apology   only
his pungent wanderer's kiss   & a stone
intended for Mother   A turquoise from somewhere
in Persia   almost

the size of a child's fist
Unlucky stone   someone tells me on the docks:
the petrified bones of those who die
of unrequited love

*   *   *

In two years   what further explanation
what claim of good intent to make amends?
None   Only the sight of him scheming
turning his back again
on the notion of home   its tiny bridges
arched like questioning eyebrows

But this time calling
back to me over his shoulder   *Come*
see for yourself what words cannot describe

1324

And what did I learn?   Only
that he was right   No words can describe
far countries to the timid   No oaths
convince them   Even now they tiptoe round my deathbed
& whisper *Renounce your lies   Go to God unburdened*
I growl that I've not told the half
of all I've seen

Through a geography of voices
alien peoples   animals   customs

woven into the Silk Road itself   a black thread
of doubt   *No one will believe this*

Men painted with flowers & animals
the true unicorn
black stones that burn
a fibre washed in fire...
all these were as fables to them
amusements for children
A merchant's hard-earned account   my prison
book   dismissed as a fine romance   Perhaps

it was   There was romance
of every kind – my father's foreign sons
were proof of that   I know where
the most beautiful women are found
& what strange hospitalities travellers
dare not decline   But I have little enough
to show for all that   Such stones as were
late for my mother soothe me as little

I go now to lie with my father
beneath his stone in San Lorenzo
to dream for all eternity
of the trading places
those knots in the Silk Road
where   huddled against the night air
we stared in silence at the dying fire
& understood each other

Pigeons, St Mark's Square

They are of one mind   one
tiny mind   They're not

elephants   not exotic or
suspected
of secret wisdom

Unlike whales
& the born-again   they will not be
saved   the Passenger already
long departed

They are only
grey Skinnerian pawns
witlessly pecking wherever
crumbs may be found
Their take-off sound is a round
of gloved applause

for Venice   the magnificent
impossibility
that mad network of sinking stones
& looking-glass roads

the archetype of Calvino's invisible cities
a three-dimensional model
of an M.C. Escher print: image
& mirror-image

They fly in his cunning patterns
of perpetual metamorphosis
the shapes they make
come apart
come together

interlock with their own
shadows   transform
into fishes & back again

complex geometric mosaics to rival
the floor of St. Mark's
which also rises & falls
with Venice   reflecting
in warped marble
its wavering fortunes

Jungfrau Tour

Jungfraujoch, Switzerland

Figurines on a toy railroad   they are
drawn   through a miracle of engineering
out of flower-strewn alpine meadows
into the dark bowels of mountains

The giggles of Japanese schoolgirls have that
delicate   music-box quality as they rise
tinkling   to *The Roof of Europe*
At intervals   these cuckoo-clock
citizens pop out
the jerked-open doors   whir
to designated spots   snap
shutters   giggle   whir
back again to their places

Mouths full of fine chocolate   at last
they arrive at the chill breath
of ice-fields   the slippery *OBSERVATION*s
the high point of souvenirs
On a dare   they run breathlessly
up the stairs   Into oxygen-
starved brains   the mountain panorama
folds itself   accordion-style   like
a packet of perfect postcards

The fattest man in Switzerland

That day you wore the blue sweater
& held tiny white flowers to your cheek
you smiled as though your reserve
was melting in the green pastures

as though your long hurt at my thoughtlessness
might not last forever   as though
maybe there was enough sun after all

with trails groomed like parkland   even the cows
clean & collared with great bells   Everything said
health   everything was müsli & pure milk –

& we stopped at the foot of the glacier
to photograph the ice   an abstract
of blue-white glass   randomly
fissured with dark earth   that later
gave us nothing

of scale   or
which way was up   or
what we were seeing   save strange
possibilities

just as young Paul Klee discovered
in the marble-topped café tables
of his uncle who he called
the fattest man in Switzerland

Threatening snowstorm

The sky swollen like yesterday's
paper lying soggy in a snow bank
sours to bruise-purple
in failing light   Soon
the threadbare cloud will split
spilling old news:
grated Dachau soap
ashes
ground bone
In loops of parallel time   Klee & I
rub our aching fingers

Bern 1937   he plays by heart
Don Giovanni's last aria   sunset
hugging the violin curves
His scleroderma is worse   In Winnipeg '65
I shovel snow   barehanded
too stubborn to go back
for gloves

A stranger is coming
a newspaper man who wants me
to call him Uncle like other boys do
Saw my picture in his paper   read
I want to be a writer   says the two of us
have lots to talk about   For him
I'm shovelling   for him my hands

are freezing   Scleroderma: degenerative
crippling a painter's hands   crippling
his music   By the time I shovel out yesterday's
blizzard   tonight's will have begun   the path
buried again   the hands

contracted to claws   *Degenerate
Art* included 17 Klee paintings
By 1940   he was dead
while the clouds above Dachau bellied
heavy with ash   My *uncle*
never showed   I didn't need him
or the choirmaster who lured me
to his place with the latest records
I kept writing to save my life
through years of skidding
out of control   Took the corner too fast
in Dad's car   Never mentioned

my narrow escapes   I was on my knees
praying   clawing my way out with bare hands
the tail lights glowing red
as small furnaces in the snow

The Child-Eater

There are traces of blood in a fairy tale
— Susan Howe

Childless ones
like you & me
dine out whenever we want

Max has never left Fiona
with a sitter   Mishearing *Bring her*
as *Leave her*   he takes me
for an ogre of selfishness
cold & cruel as anything in Grimm's

       *   *   *

Motherly women in gingerbread cottages
push hungry kids into ovens   Giants threaten
to grind young bones for bread
My father buys a baker's dozen
lets them freeze in the back porch dungeon
till he wants another

Sometimes my mother makes her own
puts a parka over the rising
to keep off drafts   It's winter
most of the year in Winnipeg
but I'm warm as toast in mine

coming rosy-cheeked & breathless
into the kitchen to say
It's like an oven in here

Something smells good   I volunteer
to lick the bowl
whatever it is   As in fairy tales
appetite precedes knowledge

        *   *   *

... precedes knowledge

A schoolgirl's misunderstanding:
if I swallow   I'll end up
with a bun in the oven

        *   *   *

Moses & I   teenage fathers
of a starving African child
try to physicalise
ethical theory   It's Winnipeg   late '60s   Should we
eat nothing but tofu & bean sprouts
like the guy two doors down
who won't wear leather shoes
or sit on his parents' couch   He knows
who died for furniture glue
whose bones are ground to make our daily bread

He wears principled black sneakers   sits
weightless on his lawn chair
the adolescent Gandhi of his living room

*   *   *

1905   Einstein clerked in the Bern patent office
his days practical   his dreams
pure   working nights on his special theory
of relativity

a fleshless physics in which
no kids turned to smoke
no bones were ground into flour   no skin
stitched into lampshades
No theory existed for these as yet

unobserved phenomena   His all-consuming curiosity
had not yet split the naïve world
to its very core   Hiroshima had not become
a furnace for innocents   Who imagined

children with intimate knowledge of ovens
except in Grimm's?   The gaping maw
of military science
no more than a yawn before bedtime

*   *   *

Winnipeg   Summer   '53   & US Army planes
dust carcinogen over ignorant
backyards   The Pentagon
lies   claiming chemical fog
might hide us from Russian
A-Bombs   In the grip of Cold
War hysteria   the mayor swallows it

Zinc cadmium sulfide   36 times
in less than a month   sifts like icing sugar
over my pregnant mother delivering
loaves from the oven   my cheering father
urges the Bombers to hit harder
When the team doctor's
paged away from the game   dad & grandfather
exchange knowing looks   That's my mother
going into labour

   * * *

My mother   for whom family
came as naturally as breathing
sees our handfasting   our fruitless
un-marriage   & despairs

She thinks restaurants
will betray us in old age
that we'll ache for sons & daughters
& be empty

We are the animal
that devours its young
that nuzzles pretty Fiona & says
I could eat you up

that threatens brats with a ravenous ogre
who crams one in his mouth   while the rest
squirm in his sack like kittens
to be drowned   In this tidy civilised city
of chocolate & neutrality   the child-eater
holds for us a perverse
fascination   like a grim collision
at the intersection of hungers
not yet named

Don't forget to write

I am disappearing, he thought
but the photographs were worth it.
                    —Anne Carson

Dear Boss   Heave except my official sigh of
resignation   I've runt off to join the circle
Donuts attempt to follow me …

The new European despondent
for DisAssociated Press
files up-to-the-minute retorts
on events of another lifetime
Dis

-jointed
-appointed
narrative   replete with beginning
muddle
& end

Forgive   John Bunyan   this pilgrim's
lack of progress

Forgive   Mary Shelley   the
Frankensteinian railway stitchery

anti-postcards
cultural junk-
mail   snapshots
of the unmonumental

cut-&-paste untraceable
ransom notes
for the Old World –

old world   old self
lost & found-poems
what the pickpocket left behind

a post office of
not-quite-dead letters

26 frames from a moving train
through some larger
blurrier landscape

details of famous paintings
glimpsed through keyholes
of locked galleries

masks insufficiently false
toys too life-like
to amuse

a collage of hand-drawn maps
to poisonous restaurants
& hotels run by
the national penal system

eavesdroppings

a Rorschach blot of
matador blood

stern warnings
misunderstood at borders

relic bones of saints & nobodies
wrestled away from dogs

torn museum tickets   admissions
of failure

First Ladies: To Ben, from bi-centennial Paris

Street barricades shield the Gorbachevs
from too much dangerous *fraternité*
He's popular here but who knows

how long he'll last   By fluke we witness the
zoom-past in the closed car   Flashback
to Winnipeg
November sixty-three

Strange schooling:
a radio on & our teacher silent
finally letting history speak for itself
A collective holding of breath   then he is dead
dead dead   For weeks TV & *Life* lay down
image-strata of communal memory
– the too-casual motorbikes   open car
then the panic   Desperate Jackie
crawling toward the trunk
Was she helping the secret
service man or escaping
the line of fire?
– Lenny Bruce's unseemly
legitimate question

At the Louvre   we sight Raisa again
caught in a crossfire
of flashbulbs   then vanishing into revolution
-nostalgia   Remember the sprint through the Louvre
in Godard's *Bande à Part*?   That spirit
lives   Hostel kids brag they 'did' Spain
in three days   Culture shock

troops with fast-food appetites   conducting
lightning raids on High Art   All summer
we're back-to-backpack in this rite
of Euro-passage   out of sync
but caught in their slipstream all the same   Off
the train at Lyon we found the hordes had rucksacked
the city   Bedless   we dashed back
mere seconds before it pulled out
Wrong year to drop in on France unannounced
Pandemonium ...

Flashback to the Philippines   Nineteen eight-one
In your kitchen we chew over supper & saving the nation   The
opposition-in-exile is Ninoy Aquino   If he dares return
he'll be swept to the Presidency   You venture that
Marcos would probably murder him first   Then you joke
how First Lady Imelda got rich in mining –
That's mine   that's mine ...   Some friends
might ask us to 'carry something' you say   I feel
tested   like Lillian Hellman in pre-war Europe

In Cebu   your pal puts us up in a hospital
where at night we hear women weep down the darkened halls
The authority of the government emanates
from the people intones a stone   Graffiti
moans *Boycott this rigged election!*   Everywhere we go
we hear the approaching motorcade
of history's latest

ugly Kodak moment   A local named Junior
chats me up *Where you from? Who you visiting?*
A clumsy puppy   bumbling
into the sightlines of my camera   Then
Imelda swans out
& it's clear he's Secret
Service

            I shot like mad
on that trip but rarely people   Never felt right
scoping their open smiles   Just once a telephoto:
'Toddler with Yellow Umbrella'   Lined him up
in my crosshairs & snapped him in fierce noon sun
The shutter click fractions second
thought – time enough for the damage   He saw the
long barrel trained on his head
& screamed   The sound of him felt like innocent
blood on my hands

Thanks to Junior I only winged Imelda
I'm no Oswald or Ron Galella with
moving targets   In such situations
a clean shot is everything   Ben   you were dead
right about Aquino – one to the head
on the airplane steps   He was
cold before he even touched the ground

The living arrive as tourists

How mundane the Munich city bus
to Dachau

& the driver who sings out our stop
like any other

though it is
& was   the last

a conceptual end point
beyond which it's impossible
to travel

*   *   *

Fenced with stars
with wire thorns
the dead wear prayer shawls
of wind

Lesions of rust & lichen
the maps of their new continents

The living arrive as tourists
from the ignorant lands of now
from cities buzzing with random noise & colour

only to have the dead walk
into their arms
& out their backs

staining them with history
with grave dirt

        *   *   *

Next day   needing to be shed
of death   we drift into shops for new clothes
fresh fruit & bread

But the ghosts persist   At the bakery door
I brush Bruno Schulz
with a warm loaf under his arm

I watch while
a Gestapo officer
shoots him to spite another
The fresh bread spattered with blood
lies broken in the gutter

It's too much   Desperate for innocence
we let a glockenspiel draw us
to the Toy Museum

only to find a troop of Aryan soldiers
stripped to the waist
flexing the muscles of the Master Race

among dismembered puppets
a Teddy Bear in armour

& a sinister wind-up fly
many times larger than life as
grotesquely disproportionate
as Nazi death –

industrial   economic
not the single bed but the showers
the ovens   not the narrow coffin
but the mass grave
crawling with mechanical flies

      *   *   *

Leaving we find on the bottom step
the crumpled ghost-body of Primo Levi
who two years ago threw himself
down a stairwell like this

Brave man   jerked
over the rail by depression
by Auschwitz-survivor guilt   or the burden
of care for his invalid mother
These past weeks   his books
have been teaching me

& today his shroud
is a bag from the men's-wear store
To my unGermanic ear   its corporate logo
rings ironic   One name
written over & over: *Theo*
Wormland

Statuary

For you I wanted to be the broad back of the cow
that man slept on outside the Munich State Museum

the graceful aching phantom limbs
of two-thousand-year-old Venus

the toes of Saint Peter
worn away by kisses

Instead I am the madman's hammer
smashing the Pietà

the x-ray of damage
& the glass that now keeps us
from touching

Backward

While we talked, a number of cities passed us,
going in the opposite direction.
                              – Grace Paley

We're travelling wrong
letting the train haul us
backward through the landscape   Coarse
dry country   lacking tender
wings of irrigation   smooth
designer shops   the drugged sweet
lethargy of beaches

Grim with factories   charged with resolute
arms of electricity   this is a region
experts tell us not to look at

It exists for them only as distance
between postcards

There are no guidebooks for the real
no joke T shirts
no Kodak film booths
& no translation

Fellow passengers insist we
stand in this backward country
while they reverse   row by row
every seat in the car

We don't know *What difference?*
in any language but our own   Satisfied
our forward-looking neighbours

let each grimy town   every dusty crop
scroll by

a backdrop   as in Hollywood car windows
where the driver pays no attention to anything
but his lines

Blood moon

The heart has broken its moorings.
      – Vicente Huidobro

First taste
of Barcelona: blood
moon Rare

as a blue one but
hot

a live coal Strange
how it draws us like a tide
into the switching yard

Raw wound
Scarlet letter
O! Gory
thumbprint after the crime

Stepping into the night
we join the mournful
uncoupling music of trains

Smudge of red chalk
on blackness: how far
our passion has drifted away

Walking therapy

Walking to Mass   it strikes me
I won't live forever
Soon I am seventy-four   though scarcely born
& all I've built seems no more
than the copper pots of my father
& his father & his father before him

Like these passing by   I was once a dandy
But that was another life   That Gaudí
is dead   Even received the last rites once
while sick with Malta fever
That blessed fever made me
a new man by grace   Thereafter
I tripled my efforts in God's name
A childhood rheumatism nags me still   But
such aches are divine reminders
of human frailty   a link
to the man I was

I've always known the expiatory church
would demand the humble labour of several lifetimes
Yet even of my share   much work remains
It was right to give up
secular commissions &
commit myself with a whole heart
to the Holy Family   Travel as a pilgrim
toward the soul's great purpose!   So daily I walked –
close to twenty years – some four & a half kilometres
When my walking partner fell ill   I lodged

in the studio & devoted the hours saved
to extra work   It reminded me that I too
was young no more   though I keep up
my walks to Mass   two more kilometres

So dies the butterfly   only to become the worm
a nondescript relic
begging the streets for his dream   Critics whine that
my old vanity now vaults heavenward   But
can they not see Creation
alive in the stone?   I tell them
God draws no straight lines   nature
flows & flowers & leaps up
supple & glorious
& the Holy Family will stand at the centre
of that flowering: schools   craft workshops
the clamour & bellow of life
& loud hosannas that hit me like a blow –

What's this?   Am I come to my communion?
I taste in my mouth
the body & the blood ...

Collage o' Picasso: On seeing *Guernica*

. . . born in Spain, died in France,
he was not afraid of baggy pants . . .

*   *   *

He was afraid
that his hair & fingernail trimmings
could be used to master him

He was afraid
to make a decision
(de-cidere: to cut off)

so his lovers overlapped
alongside the dying relationship
the one being born

*   *   *

What everyone knows of him: intense
dark eyes   Blue
Period   harlequin   Paris
Gertrude Stein

who shook him
by the lapels – *you are*
extraordinary
within your limits . . .

Women simultaneously broken down
to various angles were probably
Picasso's

Fractured faces
new forms for
old agonies   bullfights   Civil War
cubism   superimposed
planes

*   *   *

It requires an entire building to hold the horror
of his *Guernica*   twenty-five feet by eleven

Stand well back
before making a judgement   Remember he didn't stop
his two abused lovers who
came to blows over him
as he painted this

*   *   *

*Some were certainly following & were certain that the one they were
then following was one bringing out of himself then something that was
coming to be a heavy thing, a solid thing and a complete thing.*

*   *   *

Afraid

(de-cidere: to cut off)

    *   *   *

Ten years after last seeing him
she sorts among old love letters
& tissue-paper packets
of fingernail clippings

    *   *   *

When I die, it will be a shipwreck,
and as when a huge ship sinks,
many people all around
will be sucked down with it.

    *   *   *

Paulo his son
died from booze & drugs

Pablito his grandson
died after drinking
bleach

Marie-Therese his young lover
hanged herself

Jacqueline his last wife
put a bullet in her brain

       *   *   *

It required ninety-odd years
to exhaust his terrible energy

still the room can scarcely bear
all that has soaked this canvas

Stand well back

Geography

Here in Seville   near
the Court of Oranges
Magellan began turning the world
round
                    Circumnavigation:
what a globed fruit of a word!   The world
grew fuller   sweeter   more beautiful
after that   never again
flat
& tightly-horizoned

You pour over maps   half-listening
as I read from *Invisible Cities*:
spider-web cities   cities in mirrors
cities whose fickle citizens empty them
in rotation   Such destinations
elude the cartographer's grid-net   existing
in rumour   exerting on the mind
the tidal pull of the dreamed

In Winnipeg   geography
was altogether visible   Mr. Russell's Grade 10 slide show
forced-marched us into the Shield   swamped us in
soul-sucking muskeg   drilled us
in boredom's bedrock   *This is lichen ...*
he droned ... *the nickel in the picture*
gives you the scale   This is
Mrs. Russell in Sudbury ...   (the mining town's
Big Nickel confounding the scale)   Mr. Russell was
large with a small-change wife in his pocket   a puffy man

deflated by our suspect success
on The Big Test

          Locate a city ...
where trust is not disappointed   where
the silver-white nickel heart remains unalloyed
I failed you both   proved unworthy
of flat-footed steadfast map-readers

& lost my way among *Trading cities*
Cities and desire

Exhausted

Museum days: did we think we could
buy into history?

Consumers   our poisonous modernity
has eaten the Acropolis!

Our Volkswagens blacken
the bone-white monuments   shouting down
what blood has softly
insisted over centuries

*   *   *

Old woman   keeper of the Spanish tower
perches bird-like on a stool atop the first flight

her skirt weighted with coins   her eyes
patient all day with the bland new-world faces

In the clinking of silver   a message
in the motion of her hands making change:

We may have exhausted our history
but you've scarcely had one

*   *   *

Heading south   we cast off our excess
baggage   trying to lighten up   It did no good
With every step we shouldered
another burden:

                    the Inquisition
Columbus & his consequence   By Dachau
we bent double with
the weight of the dead   We wore relic
finger-bone leg irons   slept in airless rooms
like ovens   Each night we rented
fresh-laundered sheets
on which to act out
our own falsely innocent history
& woke every morning grey
with weightless ash

Travel in photographs

Before our tour ended, he had taken 4,387 pictures, although his camera had been broken for two days. It was not exactly broken; it had simply closed its eye, exhausted.

— Grace Paley

Always assessing whether that smile
in this light is beauty
worth shooting

Roll after roll of snap
decisions on the perfect angle
of memory

on the relative value of
public & private history   Now & then

surprising vision – close-ups   time
exposures   More often sour
self-loathing

that the eye has become
a meter   that

without being willed   a frame
imposes itself around innocent faces

that while the camera's dead
weight hangs round the neck like a curse

no playing child is safe
no land too holy

Spider web hat

Too dark in there
for a picture   You'll have to take
my word

>   *   *   *

Near the end   museums blur into Yeats'
rag-&-bone shop of the heart
a place of terrors

wonders   oddities   You linger
with dolls & toys
I'm drawn to masks & puppets
We lose each other

in a maze of abundant
simulacra   Doubling
back for one another   our reflections
become the exhibit

confusions
obsessions   self/ deceptions all
fleetingly revealed

>   *   *   *

In London's Museum of Mankind
they display a spider web hat

Too dark in there
for a picture   You'll have to
take my word   Frail thing
who would believe it

fashioned by a black cupid
poison-arrow Botswana bushman
hunter-gatherer
trance-dancer   The guard
wasn't looking as I knelt by the glass
to align my reflection

& feel its weightless weight
haloing my head   I took it
as transparent metaphor
while the London rain rained down
without mercy & the fine mesh of our love
fell apart in our clumsy hands

End

... old apartments saturated with the emanations of numerous existences and events ... no wonder they are susceptible to distant, dangerous dreams. The essence of furniture is unstable, degenerate, and receptive to abnormal temptations: it is then that on this sick, tired and wasted soil colourful and exuberant mildew can flourish in a fantastic growth, like a beautiful rash.

– Bruno Schulz

Apartment

Loss burns
like a naked light bulb
all through the night

The dental-drill whine of traffic
thins but never stops

a masterful torture sustained
on crick-necked   fold-out sleep
& rough jerks of dreaming

It can never be home   this
waiting room   this
ungiving shoe

The names of the months
sound to me like threats

Losing the elephant

He cannot fathom
how they could lose an elephant

Did they lose it all at once
or piece by piece?

Or did it waste away
anorexic
to the size of a horse
a dog

a cat
a mouse
licking the corners
of the bedroom
making a meal
of shadows

How could it vanish?   He's
ashamed to show his face   Carelessness
is universally despised

Behind their doors
he can hear the neighbours
whispering

Such fools!
Such utter fools!
To lose an elephant!

Memento

Garbage Monday:
running late
with stinking bag in hand
I startle a grizzled man
sifting through trash

He flashes a toothless
apologetic smile   & lifts
some grimy prize under my nose

You & the little woman? he
cackles   *Broken*
forever says my heart
from its dumpster of grief   But no

inside a matchbox on his
greasy paw we sit
two jewel-perfect miniatures
in the breakfast nook of our house

Or what was once our house   Such
amazing faithfulness
to detail!   We're making small talk
over sardines & baby peas   How faded
& dainty the curtains!   How worn
the linoleum!   Even the tap is dripping
just as it does – *must remember to fix that!*

I hear myself ask *What do you want*
for it? He scowls & spits
& snatches the treasure away
More than you've got he mutters
More than you've got!

In heaven: A resurrection dream

He shall see them again in Heaven
the cheese
the vegetable dip

the half tin of crushed
pineapple   the ancient heel
of bread   The Bible says
they also serve

who wait in the ark of winter   who are
passed over in favour of
phone-in pizza   whose *best before*
days are numbered
then forgotten

But they shall be lifted up
in the new communion   resurrected
fresher than Safeway ever dreamed   The leftovers
shall be made whole   sardines
& strawberries joined in one
bizarre divine recipe

& all will be sweet-smelling & wholesome
in the Inglis of eternal life
& there will be no more wailing &
wrinkling of the nose   no cruel clatter
& scraping of plates at the trash

no sickening grey-white mould
of unprotesting patience
as acquired in the bachelor's fridge

Prayer to the grey angel

O angel of the compromised
descend

to those who rake the ashes
of their old lives
with weeping violins

Seize us in your fierce talons
take us

out behind the woodshed
& beat out of us
the last bitter tear of self-pity

Teach us a lesson we won't forget
O sad grey angel of shame

The provisional government

History's radio analyses the fall
of Gorbachev   as the wound of
the new address
scabs over   Misguided
hope picks at it   wanting
the old life back
without a scar

Through a month of Sundays
the grit of guilt
strips the second-hand table
through colour after colour   down to
raw wood

On the fine sand of this penance
a shaky provisional government
bolstered by subscriptions
an ironing board
the five kilo bag of flour

Thus the state of emergency
passes   The unmiraculous saints –
laundry
garbage
rent
– get days named after them
The clock resumes its
indifferent circles   its predictable
outbursts of alarm   Order
if not quite happiness
is restored

Notes on the Text

Title
In landscape architecture, 'desire lines' are features that develop as people choose their own paths across an area rather than those laid out by the designers.

Beginning
The epigraph is from Bruno Schulz's *Street of Crocodiles*.

Cliché Europe
The phrase "history and its near relative histrionics" is from Graham Swift's novel *Waterland*.

Muddle
The epigraph, which describes a method of 'inverting' objects using prisms, is taken from a 1956 letter published in *M.C. Escher: His Life and Complete Graphic Work*, edited by J.L. Locher.

Black Thread
Canadian poet, fiction writer and editor Bronwen Wallace died of oral cancer in 1989.

Freud was diagnosed with oral cancer in 1923, underwent treatments over many years, and eventually died of his disease in 1939. His remark "My prosthesis doesn't speak French" is quoted in *The Life and Work of Sigmund Freud* by Ernest Jones.

Richard Blessing was a Seattle poet and prose writer who died of brain cancer in 1983.

Brazilian composer Heitor Villa-Lobos was diagnosed with bladder cancer in 1948. Treated surgically, he was well for 11 years, but died of related complications in 1959. His answer to the question "Are you composing?" is quoted in the CBC Radio documentary, *The Indian in the Tuxedo*.

Humblessed
St Francis of Assisi received the stigmata during a vision in 1224. St Clare's order received 'the privilege of poverty' – permission to live wholly on alms – in 1215, and is now known as the Poor Clares.

Threatening Snowstorm
Scleroderma is "a collagen disease ...causing contracture and deformities of joints and widespread systemic effects". Diagnosed in 1935, Klee died of it five years later.

In 1937, Joseph Goebbels confiscated from German museums 16,000 modern artworks unacceptable to the Reich. Better-known pieces were sold abroad; many others were burned. An exhibit of this 'Degenerate Art', including works by Chagall, Ernst, Kandinsky, Mondrian, and Klee, opened in Munich May 21st, 1937.

The Child-Eater
The *kindlifresserbrunnen* or Child-eater Fountain, was designed by sixteenth-century artist Hans Gieng. It stands in the Kornhausplatz in Bern, Switzerland.

The US Army conducted simulated germ warfare tests in Winnipeg between July 9 and August 1 of 1953, using the carcinogen zinc cadmium sulfide, but lied to civic officials about the purpose of the tests. Pentagon scientists insist they used harmless quantities of the naturally-occurring chemical.

Handfasting is "a form of irregular or trial marriage ceremonialised by a joining of hands".

First Ladies
Senator Benigno 'Ninoy' Aquino was assassinated by military officers in Manila in 1983. His widow Corazon 'Cory' Aquino subsequently led a non-violent revolution that drove out dictator Ferdinand Marcos and his First Lady and Housing Minister, Imelda Marcos. Granted asylum in the U.S, Ferdinand died there in 1989. Imelda returned to the Philippines in 1991 and re-entered politics.

Ron Galella was infamous for persistent attempts to photograph Jacqueline Kennedy Onassis and her children in private life.

Threatening Snowstorm
Takes its title from a Klee painting.

Walking Therapy
Antonio Gaudí's Cathedral of the Holy Family, begun in 1883, remains under construction today. To combat rheumatism, the architect ate a vegetarian diet, had special bathing habits, used homoeopathic medicines, and regularly took long walks. He died in 1926, struck by a streetcar while walking to Mass. Several taxi drivers, not recognising him, refused to take him to hospital, assuming he was an indigent.

Collage o' Picasso
The quotations, in order, come from: the song 'Picasso's Mandolin' by Guy Clark; Arianna Huffington, in *Picasso: Creator and Destroyer*; Gertrude Stein, quoted by Huffington; Gertrude Stein, in her *Three Portraits of Painters*; Picasso, quoted by Huffington.

The Living Arrive as Tourists
Schulz was a teacher, artist and fiction writer in south-eastern Poland. His short story collection, *Cinnamon Shops*, appeared in 1934, and was reprinted in the US under the title *Street of Crocodiles*. He was shot in the street by a Gestapo officer in 1942.

Primo Levi wrote many books on his Auschwitz experience. He committed suicide in 1987.

Statuary

The *Rindermarktbrunnen*, or cattle market fountain, by Josef Henselmann stands near the Munich State Museum. The Venus de Milo is in the Louvre. Klee noted the eroded statue of St Peter in the October 31, 1901 entry of his Italian travel diary. Michelangelo's Pietà was attacked in 1972 and is now behind glass.

End

The epigraph is from *Street of Crocodiles* by Bruno Schulz.

Apartment

The quotation is from 'Widower's Tango' by Pablo Neruda, translated by W.S. Merwin.

Formerly a social worker in cancer care, Glen Downie was 1999 Writer-in-Residence at the Medical Humanities Program of Dalhousie University's Faculty of Medicine. He has published four books of poetry, co-edited the work-writing anthology *More Than Our Jobs*, and appeared in various literary, medical and general interest periodicals, including *The Globe & Mail, The Lancet, The Malahat Review, Rampike* and *Prism international*.